Titles in the series

Celebrity Court Cases
Celebrity Stalkers
Crime Scene Investigation
Crystal Meth
CSI: Case Studies
Dangerous Dogs
Deadly Mission
Hurricane Katrina Survival Stories
Hurricane Hell
Identity Theft
Inside the War in Afghanistan
Killer Flu
Most Wanted Terrorists
Plastic Surgery Case Studies
Plastic Surgery Gone Wrong
Terrorism: The Homeland Threat
Wrongfully Accused

www.amazingstoriesbooks.com

LATE-BREAKING
AMAZING STORIES™

ROAD RAGE
An epidemic of fury

by Roberta McDonald

PUBLISHED BY ALTITUDE PUBLISHING LTD.
1500 Railway Avenue, Canmore, Alberta T1W 1P6
www.amazingstoriesbooks.com
1-800-957-6888

Copyright 2006 © Roberta McDonald
All rights reserved
First published 2006

Extreme care has been taken to ensure that the information contained in this book is accurate and up to date at the time of printing. However, neither the author nor the publisher is responsible for errors, omissions, loss of income or anything else that may result from the information contained in this book.

All web site URLs mentioned in this book were correct at the time of printing. The publisher is not responsible for the content of external web sites or changes that may have occurred since publication.

In order to make this book as universal as possible, all currency is shown in U.S. dollars.

Publisher	Stephen Hutchings
Associate Publisher	Kara Turner
Canadian Editors	Deborah Lawson & Frank MacKay
U.S. Editor	Julian S. Martin

We acknowledge the financial support of the Government of Canada through the Book Publishing Industry Development Program (BPIDP) for our publishing activities.

ALTITUDE GREENTREE PROGRAM
Altitude Publishing will plant twice as many trees as were used in the manufacturing of this product.

Cataloging in Publication Data

McDonald, Roberta
    Road rage / Roberta McDonald.

(Late breaking amazing stories)
Includes bibliographical references.
ISBN 1-55265-310-2 (U.S. ed.)
ISBN 1-55439-514-3 (Canadian ed.)

    1. Road rage. I. Title. II. Series.

TL152.3.M33 2005a	363.12'51	C2005-905778-5 (U.S. ed.)
TL152.3.M33 2005	363.12'51	C2005-905769-6 (Canadian ed.)

In Canada, Amazing Stories® is a registered trademark of Altitude Publishing Canada Ltd. An application for the same trademark is pending in the U.S.

Printed and bound in Canada by Friesens
2 4 6 8 9 7 5 3 1

"When someone smiles or waves at you, you remember their humanity. When someone honks at you, you remember their license number."

William Hubbard, researcher

CONTENTS

	Photographs	8
1	Two Worlds Shatter	15
2	Insights into Road Rage	25
3	Road Rage Case Studies	48
4	Road Rage Around the World	77
5	Celebrities and Road Rage	84
6	Efforts to Reduce Road Rage	99
7	Tips for Avoiding Road Rage	109
8	Looking Ahead—Theories and Suggestions	120
	Timeline	123
	What Others Say	125
	Amazing Facts and Figures	129

ROAD RAGE

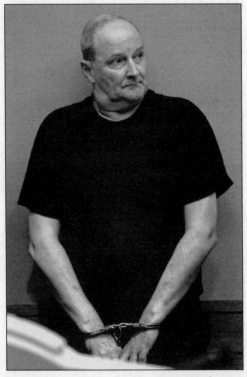

Walter Bishop, 60, stands in court in August 2005. Bishop was held without bail after pleading innocent to fatally shooting another man in a case of road rage. For more on the story, see Chapter 3.

PHOTOGRAPHS

Sara McBurnett is seen sitting with her white bichon frise, Leo, in an undated photo. People across the United States donated reward money to help find the dog's killer.

In 2001, Andrew Burnett, 27, was found guilty of killing the little dog in a case of road rage and sentenced to three years in prison. See page 59 for the story.

The tragic result of a road rage incident, Texas Department of Public Safety officers stand near the accident site of two vehicles on Interstate 20 near Canton, Texas, December 28, 2005. A state trooper called the accident "a classic case of road rage," which tragically left two people dead and two more hospitalized. Jason Youngblood, 32, of Fort Worth, Texas, was charged in connection with the accident.

PHOTOGRAPHS

U.S. heavyweight boxer Mike Tyson raises his arms in victory after a fight in Copenhagen in 2001. Tyson has suffered from rage issues. For more on his story, see page 88.

Jeffrey Pattinson points to O.J. Simpson during the first day of Simpson's road rage trial, October 18, 2001, in Miami. The two sides offered starkly different versions of the December 4 encounter between Simpson and Pattinson. For the story, see page 85.

PHOTOGRAPHS

O.J. Simpson, center, flanked by his attorneys Yale Galanter, left, and Lee Cohn, right, reacts as he hears the verdict in his road rage trial, in October 2001. Simpson was acquitted of all charges resulting from a roadside confrontation the previous year.

CHAPTER 1

Two Worlds Shatter

On a blistering July day in 1987, Albert Morgan and his wife were on their way to the Orange County fairgrounds for an afternoon at the rodeo when they found themselves stuck in slow-moving traffic on the famously congested Costa Mesa Freeway in Southern California. The 18-mile (30 km) long north-south highway links Newport Beach and Anaheim. Before long, the 33-year-old Morgan had had enough of watching other cars pass him on the shoulder. It infuriated him to watch helplessly as other drivers ignored the rules of the road and tried to beat the jam. The oppressive heat, combined with the rum he had consumed earlier in the day, stoked his anger as he and his wife sat in their truck.

As Morgan's temper approached the boiling point, Paul Nussbaum was in the process of moving his Datsun onto the shoulder of the same freeway, so he could safely check some directions he'd been given. An energetic young man, Nussbaum was an avid runner with aspirations of completing a marathon. But that afternoon, the 28-year-old, who had just completed his master's degree in social work at the University of Southern California, was on his way to a barbeque at his best friend's house to celebrate.

As time inched by and traffic stood stubbornly still, Morgan's simmering frustration boiled over into rage. When he saw Nussbaum

TWO WORLDS SHATTERED

driving slowly on the shoulder, he assumed the young man was attempting to bypass the gridlocked traffic. Exploding, Morgan reached over to the glove compartment of his black Ford truck where he kept a loaded .22-caliber pistol. He pointed the revolver toward the Datsun. With his wife screaming at him to stop, he pulled the trigger, aiming toward the car he thought was passing illegally.

But his bullet didn't whiz in front of the car as Morgan had planned. Instead, it went straight through the side window, striking Nussbaum just behind the ear.

Ripping through his neck, the bullet destroyed Nussbaum's vertebrae and damaged his spinal cord, instantly and permanently changing the future he had envisioned for himself. But he didn't know he'd been shot until he awoke in a hospital, where emergency room doctors told him he had suffered a serious head wound.

The July 18 shooting made national news and remains one of the most high-profile road-rage incidents in Orange County. In the movie *LA Story*, Steve Martin makes light of the disturbing trend, and jokes about open shooting days on the freeway. But for Nussbaum and Morgan, the reality was no laughing matter.

Their lives were forever impacted by the events of that day. Both men now have a bleak view of the world.

Morgan served five years in prison after a jury found him guilty of attempted voluntary manslaughter. "I knew I was guilty," he told a reporter from the *Orange County Register* nearly 20 years later. "I accepted it." He blames his alcoholism, adding that in his booze-addled state he could have justified anything. He doesn't recall being angry enough to deliberately shoot Nussbaum. "I honestly thought I was going to shoot in front of the Datsun, and that he'd see this bullet fly by, and that it would be a warning shot," Morgan said. "That was how messed-up my thinking was."

The bullet that struck Nussbaum caused

irreversible damage. At first, he was undaunted by his prognosis and vigorously pursued rehabilitation, but after awhile Nussbaum realized he would never walk again. The young man who had once dreamed of running marathons and planned to pursue a career in social work is now confined to a wheelchair, dependent on a caregiver to meet his daily needs. He is not able to use the toilet by himself and can't get in and out of bed without assistance. His parents check in on him nearly every day.

The pain of living with a gunshot injury has been unbearable. Discussing the agony he lives with every day, he comments, "I don't want to die, but I don't want to live like this." In the early 1990s, Nussbaum became despondent and corresponded with Dr. Jack Kevorkian, the controversial doctor who champions euthanasia for terminally ill patients. In an interview for *New Mobility* magazine, Nussbaum spoke about the impact of his loss, which he feels continually, living in a wheelchair. He also shared the letter he wrote to Dr. Kevorkian in 1992. "Nothing is normal," he wrote. "Every day I live with humiliation, complete dependency on others, the chronic turnover of personal care attendants and the loss of my freedom. Death is an enviable option." The Michigan doctor agreed to help Nussbaum, but the plan fell through when physician-assisted suicide became a felony.

Nussbaum now has enough mobility to operate a computer mouse and spends about four hours a day on the Internet. He uses his computer as a fundraising resource and has personally raised between $200,000 and $250,000 for spinal-cord injury research. He also talks to others with similar injuries, offering his experience and guidance. Nussbaum says these activities have given him a purpose. Still, life doesn't get any easier.

Nussbaum has no expectation that he will ever receive the $8 million civil judgment he was awarded in court, and claims he doesn't often think about Morgan. "Only when I hear about another freeway shooting," he said. "I'm trying to forget about him and move on with the rest of my life." But he's not ready yet to forgive Morgan for shattering his hopes and dreams.

Even though the two men have never met or spoken to each other, they both say insanity on the freeways is bound to ruin more lives. There have been at least a dozen freeway shootings in Southern California since mid-March of 2005. Nussbaum believes the ongoing violence on the road is a result of sociopathic tendencies, and he worries for the safety of other drivers. He compares the present attitude of drivers to the old frontier days, calling California the "wild, wild West."

After serving his time and reflecting on the events of that day, Morgan is remorseful. He says his time in prison made him realize the stupidity of his actions. He admits that it was "an idiotic act" that not only destroyed Nussbaum's life and that of the young man's family, but also fragmented his own family and made him an outcast. Disgusted by his actions, Morgan's wife left him. Many of his relatives disowned him. He received numerous death threats and was completely ostracized from his community.

Now 50, Morgan suffers from an inherited disease that claimed both of his kidneys after he was released from prison in 1993. His blood must now be purified three days a week by a kidney dialysis machine, and he is too sick to work.

Morgan has some advice for motorists who are wound up and ready to snap. He cautions drivers to slow down and take a moment to consider the consequences of their actions. He also advocates meditation and deep-breathing

> **FOR INFORMATION LEADING TO THE ARREST...**
>
> In just over four weeks in the spring of 2005, four people were shot and killed in road-rage incidents in California's Orange County. The attacks sparked such a wave of fear that Los Angeles city council began issuing rewards of up to $60,000 for information leading to the arrest of road-rage attackers.
>
> *Source: Orange County Register*

ORANGE COUNTY, CALIFORNIA: SHOOTINGS AT A GLANCE, JANUARY–APRIL 2006

January 7, 2006
A woman unwittingly found herself in the middle of a raging traffic dispute between two other drivers and was caught in the crossfire. After being shot, she drove herself to the hospital where she was treated and released.

January 24, 2006
After an "unsafe lane change," two Anaheim men were fatally shot on the Riverside freeway.

March 14, 2006
A 22-year-old Santa Ana man was sentenced to 50 years in prison after he fatally shot Mike Decker on the freeway following a high-speed altercation involving shouting and raised middle fingers. Decker was unarmed.

April 7, 2006
Following a brief fistfight, a 60-year-old candy machine vendor stabbed a 26-year-old man in the stomach. The injured man required hospitalization.

Source: Orange County Register

techniques to control angry impulses. From the wisdom he acquired at great personal cost, he warns, "Control your temper. I know better."

CHAPTER 2

Insights into Road Rage

The term "road rage" is believed to have been coined by the U.S. media, originally to describe the most violent events occurring between individuals while driving. Although media references currently seem to refer to all instances of aggressive driving as road rage, the New York State police point out an important difference.

What is aggressive driving?

Aggressive driving refers to any display of aggression by a driver. The New York State police define an aggressive driver as one who operates a motor vehicle in a selfish, bold, or pushy manner, without regard for the rights or safety of the other users of the streets and highways.

Although the term "aggressive driving" is often used to describe more extreme acts of physical assault that result from disagreements between drivers, it does not include using a vehicle as a weapon, physically assaulting a driver, or purposely damaging someone else's vehicle. These acts are criminal offenses, and there are laws to deal with these violent crimes.

Aggressive driving covers a wide range of other dangerous driving patterns (many of which, however, are also components of road rage). Speeding, tailgating, passing illegally on the right, weaving in and out of traffic, failing to yield the right-of-way, running red lights, cutting off other drivers, and/or any combination of these actions are widely considered aggressive driving. Making rude hand gestures, yelling, flashing high-beam headlights, and honking horns also fall within the definition.

Aggressive driving on the increase

Part of the problem may be the roads themselves. North America's highways are more crowded than ever before. A steadily increasing number of vehicles use the roads, and the number of vehicle-miles driven each year is up about 35 percent in the last 10 years. Yet, the number of miles of roadway has increased by only one percent. As well, many people believe the pace of life has increased; that everyone is busier. When people feel their time is at a premium, road congestion only adds to the build-up of daily frustration.

According to the media, public highways are becoming the stage for an increasing number of aggressive-driving or road-rage events, and the problem has created growing concern among

> **ROAD RAGE HOT SPOT**
>
> As of January 2006, Washington, DC, had the most cases of road rage in the United States.
>
> *Source: Monkeymeter.com*

motorists. The American Automobile Association (AAA), Potomac Club, commissioned a survey in early 1996 to determine which issues were of concern to drivers in Washington, DC, and area. Forty percent of drivers (the largest group) identified "aggressive drivers" as the major traffic safety threat.

No gasoline required

In Canada, given stricter gun laws and a lower density of road traffic, cases of road rage are not nearly as frequent or violent as those in the United States. However, it's still a hot topic among drivers—and road rage doesn't always have to take place between the drivers of motorized vehicles. In January 2006, an incident illustrated how little it can take to spark an altercation.

In the hustle and bustle of the inner city Kensington Market neighborhood in Toronto,

Canada, narrow streets are more conducive to walking than driving. It's not a good place for drivers in a hurry. But bicycle couriers, with their greater mobility, abound. On any given business day, there are scores of these delivery agents, gaining ground on both vehicular and pedestrian traffic.

Blogs have sprouted up on the Internet about an incident involving a beef sandwich, a female bike courier, and an agitated minivan driver. The courier claimed the minivan driver threw his beef-on-a-bun out the window of his vehicle. Offended at this act of littering, she collected the refuse from the street and tossed it back into his van. The man, enraged at her audacity, leapt out of his vehicle, shoved her and then began stomping on her bike. After several bystanders pulled him off, he got back in his van and drove away. But he soon realized his vehicle had been scratched, allegedly by her bike key. He returned to the scene, where he lunged at the courier again.

A passing photographer captured the entire incident, and the pictures are now widely available on the Internet. The courier chose not to press charges because police told her she could face mischief charges for the damage caused by her key.

The encounter between the affronted bike courier and the antagonized minivan driver is just one example of a rising trend. The number of frustrated drivers is undoubtedly on the rise in North America. However, we may not lead the road-rage pack. A July

---

CANADIANS LOOK TO THE LAW

Calgary, Alberta, is Canada's fastest growing city. In 2005, police there began sending warning letters to drivers whose bad behavior behind the wheel had been reported to the authorities by other drivers via cell phone.

Between 1993 and 2003, the number of vehicles on Ontario roads jumped nearly 50 percent, and there are now more cars per capita in Vancouver, British Columbia, than in Los Angeles. Legislation introduced in 2002 reserved the left lane of all Canadian highways for passing traffic in an effort to reduce road-rage incidents.

Source: CBC

2005 study conducted by Synovate, a leading market research firm, found that South Africa has the dubious honor of the highest reported number of road-rage incidents.

A poll conducted by ABC news and *Time* magazine on February 15, 2005, found that the average U.S. driver spends 40 hours per year—an entire, average work week—stuck in traffic. With all the stops, starts, and seemingly endless traffic-light delays, it's no surprise that people are becoming increasingly stressed. Sixty-two percent of drivers polled admitted to having feelings of frustration. Fifty-six percent frequently experienced nervousness. Forty-three percent said they often felt angry behind the wheel. Conversely, however, close to two-thirds of drivers surveyed said they felt independent on the

---

TRAFFIC SNARLS

According to the U.S. Department of Transportation, a whopping 5.7 billion work hours are lost due to traffic delays.

Source: ABC/Time Magazine Poll, "A Look Under the Hood of a Nation on Wheels," February 15, 2005

ROAD RAGE SYMPTOMS

- speeding
- aggressive acceleration
- tailgating
- weaving in and out of traffic
- excessive flashing of headlights
- excessive sounding of vehicle's horn
- rude gestures
- verbal abuse and/or threats
- deliberately hitting another person, vehicle, or object with a vehicle
- deliberately hitting another person, vehicle, or object with a weapon
- threatening to use, or using, a firearm
- engaging in pursuit of another vehicle for retaliation, or to revenge a perceived slight

road, and nearly half indicated that they felt relaxed while driving.

The biggest spike in driver frustration and aggression has occurred in large urban centers. Life in the city comes at a cost. Sixty percent of respondents to the ABC/*Time* poll who reside in densely populated cities rated their particular driving conditions as "always or generally bad." On a good day, the average commute time came in at 19 minutes, but on a bad day, it took 46 minutes. The poll found that 14 percent of Americans have changed or left a job in order to avoid a long drive to work. The majority of respondents reported having observed poor driving behaviors or habits, with 82 percent claiming to have seen other motorists speeding. Close to two-thirds reported they had witnessed inattentive drivers and 64 percent stated that they had seen aggressive driving. Twenty-seven percent reported witnessing some form of road rage in their travels.

In their book *Road Rage to Road Wise,* Dr. John Larson and Carol Rodriguez point out that most drivers would rather avoid a confrontation. They believe most angry drivers don't act on their feelings; rather, they simply stew in their cars, unnoticed. But rather than blaming this simmering anger on poorly planned infrastructure or other drivers, the authors place the

NHTSA STUDIES

The National Highway Traffic Safety Administration recently completed a U.S.-wide survey about speeding and other unsafe driving actions. The goal of the study was to determine driver attitudes about speeding and other unsafe driving behaviors, the situations in which these occur, the characteristics of unsafe drivers, and possible countermeasures. The telephone survey involved 6,000 drivers of all ages. Drivers were asked a variety of questions, including the conditions under which they exhibit unsafe driving behaviors or exceed the speed limits and the reasons why they do it.

The following results were selected from that survey:
- 62 percent said the behavior of another driver has been a threat to them in the last year.
- 36 percent listed another driver cutting in front of them as a threatening behavior.
- 75 percent felt that it was important to do something about unsafe drivers.
- 33 percent reported that they felt driving is more dangerous now than a year ago.
- 23 percent reported driving 10 mph (16 km/h) or more over the speed limit on an interstate in the previous week.
- 52 percent were satisfied with current amounts of police enforcement of red-light running.
- 50 percent were satisfied with enforcement of speed limits.
- 61 percent said there was too little enforcement of tailgating.

Source: National Conference of State Legislatures web site, "Aggressive Driving: Background and Overview Report," January 2000

blame squarely with the individual. "The major responsibility for driver anger lies with the driver, not the highway," the authors say.

Brimming with aggression

Our overall stress levels soar as our cities grow and become increasingly congested. Drivers in particular appear to be feeling more frustrated than ever. Reports of road rage are now a staple part of our media diet. On a daily basis, we read of vehicle operators lashing out at one another, sometimes displaying violent reactions to seemingly minor driving irritations. Are we losing control of our emotions? The simple answer seems to be yes.

Aaron Smelski is a psychologist who counsels patients from all walks of life. He says road rage comes up frequently as a topic during therapy sessions. In the six years he has been a counselor, Smelski has noticed a prevailing sense of powerlessness around the issue. He points out that we tend to consider our vehicles as places

> **URBAN MENTALITY**
>
> Georg Simmel, a pioneer in urban sociology, suggests that the increased concentration and diversity of people in cities puts urbanites under a particular type of stress called *cognitive overload*. This is considered to be the major cause of *urban mentality*, which is characterized by detachment from others, self-centeredness, and a calculating mind.

where we *should* feel in control, but do not. He believes this perceived lack of control, which a great number of drivers experience, could be traced directly to the search for fulfillment outside of ourselves.

According to *MonkeyMeter.com*'s Rob Campbell, 40,000 vehicular deaths occur annually on the highways and byways of the United States. The World Health Organization predicts that fatal traffic accidents will surpass HIV/AIDS-related deaths world-wide by 2020.

In his 1995 paper on road rage, Matthew Joint, head of behavioral analysis for the AAA's group policy road safety unit, points out that it is instinctual to show anger when threatened. He says we are territorial and that safe personal space is essential to our sense of well-being. When people invade our physical territory by standing too close to us, North Americans are socialized to be defensive. Joint suggests that on increasingly crowded roads, the resultant shrinking distance between cars translates into an invasion of our personal space. So, when one car cuts in front of another, or edges too close to another, those same defensive instincts take over. Many people rationalize this kind of protective behavior, calling it "defensive driving" when they cut off another driver or refuse to let someone pass. But Joint concluded that a tense situation is usually diffused when cars move away from each other.

Not all accidents can be attributed specifically to road rage, but a significant number are directly related to speed. Many drivers don't realize that excessive driving speeds, combined with hostility, make for a dangerous concoction.

Hawaii-based psychiatrist Dr. Leon James has been studying driving behaviors since 1997.

Along with Diane Nahl, James is a coauthor of *Road Rage and Aggressive Driving: Steering Clear of Highway Warfare,* which is a "how-to"—or, more accurately, a "how-not-to"—guide to driving. He recommends a series of self-awareness exercises that could prevent a moment of anger from erupting into a full-blown volcano.

James says the fundamental factors present in cases of road rage are a feeling of elevated anger, accompanied by mental violence and the desire to punish or retaliate. He notes that as we become more competitive in our day-to-day lives, driving becomes a matter of who can get to the finish line first. Whether it's a drive to the grocery store, the office, or a sporting

> **DR. JAMES'S DRIVER PERSONALITY MAKEOVER**
>
> **Step 1**
> Work on your feelings—Acknowledge that you are out of control at the wheel.
>
> **Step 2**
> Work on your thoughts—Witness yourself behind the wheel.
>
> **Step 3**
> Work on your actions—Modify yourself one step at a time.

event, arriving early (or first) is akin to winning. He says drivers climb behind the wheel and treat their daily commute more like a Formula One race than a social responsibility. This rabid desire to beat the competition results in misdirected anger and resentment.

Dr. James suggests that almost all of the driver error that leads to road accidents can be traced to insufficient "emotional intelligence," or awareness, behind the wheel. However, he believes all drivers have the capability of acquiring the necessary emotional intelligence. Paying attention to, and controlling, our mental state while driving is the key to preventing emotional outbursts, according to Dr. James. Moreover, he insists that "venting" is not as healthy as many people seem to think. "You create a cycle. You repeatedly make yourself feel worse," he says, adding that if this habit isn't checked in its initial stages, it eventually morphs into part of the psyche and can become addictive.

In his book, Dr. James discusses a number of factors that contribute to the volatile patterns seen in today's drivers.

- Being trapped in a stifling, enclosed space can lead to an outburst.
- Being unable to stretch one's legs can lead to a feeling of being caged, often resulting in an increase in blood pressure.
- The feeling of encroachment by the increasing number of vehicles can overwhelm drivers who feel a growing threat to their ability to protect their own personal space.
- Many drivers have the sense that their cars are their temples; anyone who threatens their vehicle is perceived as the enemy, a mindset that supports defensive hostility.
- Frustration results from sitting in snarled traffic, immobilized in a vehicle that is meant to provide ease of movement and freedom.

Loss of personal control is also a notable factor in increased stress levels. For example, drivers are continually being told the speeds at which they can drive; the lanes from which they are allowed to turn; and where they can, or (as is more often the case) can't, park. A sense of rebellion may set in. A feeling of "you're not the boss of me" takes hold and acting out ensues.

Another factor is the reality that varied cultures converge on our busy roads. The social differences in driving styles become apparent. Someone from Panama may be accustomed to using his or her horn as a signal, which may anger a driver from Canada who may be easily rattled by the blaring sound. Stopping to let a pedestrian cross may seem like common courtesy for one driver and utter lunacy to another.

Being in a car can also be an isolating experience. Lack of direct communication may lead to misunderstandings. For example, a driver may wave to another driver to signal a thank-you for allowing him or her onto the freeway, and the gesture is interpreted as being "flipped the bird" instead, resulting in an altercation.

In our busy society, multitasking may be

considered a necessity for getting through the workday. However, when a driver's concentration is divided between a cell phone conversation, checking a map unfolded in the front seat, and balancing a cup of steaming hot coffee wedged between the legs, too many things are

---

YOUTH AND RAGE

Is it true that young men are more prone to road rage because of anger management issues, surging hormones, and bravado?

In 2005, the Canadian Psychiatric Association released the results of a telephone survey, *Are Our Patients Driving Angry?* The study determined that, of those polled, men with the youngest average age were in the group most likely to exhibit signs of aggression, such as damaging other cars and being involved in verbal and physical confrontations. Dubbed "hard-core ragers," they also represented the smallest number (5.5 percent) of respondents.

Dr. David Lewis, who first popularized the term "iceberg road rage," claims younger men are more prone to acts of violence on the road due in part to their inability to harness their emotions. Add to this the powerful cars they tend to choose, and the result is a potentially lethal combination.

going on at once. Eating while driving has become so commonplace, it's now referred to as "dashboard dining." It's a recipe for disaster.

Denying wrongdoing is another way in which drivers relinquish responsibility for their aggressive actions. Most people consider themselves good drivers, and will usually point at the other motorist when asked who was to blame for a fender-bender.

> **DRIVING SCARED**
>
> In an online poll found at *MonkeyMeter.com*, 52 percent of drivers said they lock their doors while driving, while 43 percent admitted to getting aggravated each time they climb behind the wheel. According to this poll, the worst time of day for road rage is 3 p.m. Thursday is the worst day, with Tuesday ranking a close second. Seasonally, January is the hot month for road rage.
>
> *Source: Monkeymeter.com*

Negative attitudes toward others and an overly critical perspective lead to a lack of understanding and a willingness to shrug off or ignore valid complaints.

In a study conducted in Missouri, patients who had gone to the emergency room following car accidents were questioned about their level of anger at the time of the incidents. They were asked to rate each of several emotions on a scale of 1 to 5, indicating how irritable, angry, or hostile they had felt during the incident. The 2,446 patients were compared with 1,533 randomly selected community residents interviewed by phone. Among the injured patients, 11.8 percent reported having experienced definite anger just before being injured, with 18.2 percent saying they had been feeling at least a little angry. Overt feelings of hostility were claimed by eight percent, with 13.2 percent saying they had been feeling at least some degree of hostility. One-third reported some degree of irritability. From this survey, it would seem that a peeved driver is an accident waiting to happen.

To supplement a nationwide survey, Egg Motor Insurance of the United Kingdom conducted a unique experiment in 2002 using a driving simulator. Before the test began, half of the participants were made to feel angry and

MENTAL STATES

In Curt Rich's book, *Drive to Survive,* the author identifies four mental states.

Condition White:
Overly relaxed and unaware of your surroundings. Feeling a thousand miles away and tired, dead tired. A false sense of security makes this a hazardous way to drive.

Condition Yellow
Relaxed and aware. You are purposefully engaged in the act of driving. This is the optimum condition in which to drive.

Condition Orange
Alert and guarded. Aware of a potential threat, on the "lookout." The potential for conflict is present and you are prepared to defend yourself. Many drivers spend most of their time on the road in this hyper-vigilant condition.

Condition Red
Attack in progress. Adrenaline is surging, and the need to protect your life is top priority. Raise the alarm! This is the most dangerous condition in which to drive.

began the test with elevated adrenaline levels. The other half of the group was allowed to begin the test in a calm state of mind. After 20 minutes, one-third of those in the pre-agitated group were so flustered and hot under the collar that they lost control and smashed their virtual vehicles. Two-thirds of the group exceeded the speed limit, drove too fast for weather conditions or crowded road conditions, and tailgated other vehicles. The half of the volunteers who began the test with a level head drove in a safe, respectful manner.

In the age of "me," thinking outside of ourselves is on the decline and it's becoming increasingly common to blame incidents on the other driver. Dr. Phil McGraw, the television advice guru and advocate of self-responsibility, insists road rage stems from an inflated sense of ego and lack of empathy for other drivers. On his web site, *drphil.com*, he offers straightforward advice for dealing with simmering anger. "We live in an over-crowded, over-stressed world

INSIGHTS INTO ROAD RAGE

> ### ROAD RAGE ONLINE
>
> A plethora of road rage web sites exist. When Rob Campbell started his web site, *MonkeyMeter.com*, he felt his own driving habits were out of control. As the driver for a medical supply company, he spent over 100 hours per week on the road. The stress of Northern California's famous traffic snarls was getting to be too much for him, and he realized that he was feeling flustered and angry on a daily basis. So he took action. He started a web site, and in the process, found that most of his fellow drivers were in the same boat. As well, the scope of his job changed, so he now rides his bike to work.

with traffic jams, rude people and screaming kids. Expect some blips. If you don't expect everyone to be on your schedule, then you won't be upset when they're not." He suggests the most important way to avoid road rage is to think outside the self, bluntly advising people, "Stop thinking the world revolves around you."

CHAPTER 3

Road Rage Case Studies

Blood on Main Street—
Fury erupts in the suburbs

Residents were hurrying to work or to do shopping errands along the main drag of a sleepy Boston suburb as Sandro Andrade, a new father who had moved to the United States to be an engineer, headed for the employment office with his daughter, Alexandria, strapped into her car seat. Meanwhile, Walter Bishop, a well-liked ex-soldier, was driving his wife to the train station. On that sultry summer morning, everything seemed routine. Until their minor fender-bender on a quiet side street of Brockton, Massachusetts, the two men had never met.

Andrade was a recent immigrant from the Cape Verde islands, located in the Atlantic Ocean just off the coast of Senegal in North Africa. His dream of becoming an engineer had led him to immigrate to the United States, where he and his girlfriend, Annabella Fernandez, and their daughter, Alexandria, lived with Andrade's 75-year-old father, Artur. Sandro Andrade was known in the community as a diligent worker with a strong sense of family values, who pulled double shifts at local gas stations in order to earn money for his education.

Bishop's neighbors described him as an upstanding member of the community, the kind of guy you would wave to on the street. A former serviceman, he was well trained in the use of firearms. For 30 years, he had worked as a private security guard and had no previous criminal record.

After Andrade allegedly bumped the back of Bishop's truck, the two men got out of their vehicles and a verbal altercation ensued. Andrade raised his voice and yelled expletives at Bishop and his wife. As the quarrel ended, Andrade scribbled down Bishop's license plate number before speeding off toward the main drag. Bishop says his wife was frightened by Andrade's angry words.

Moments after Bishop dropped off his wife, he spotted Andrade's SUV in front of the employment office. He slammed on his brakes and, with tires squealing, piloted his vehicle across several lanes of traffic to attack Andrade, who was bent over, unbuckling baby Alexandria from her car seat. Using his Chevy Blazer as a battering ram, Bishop struck Andrade's smaller Isuzu. Then, without warning, the sound of gunfire echoed around the street.

"Pop! Pop! Pop! Pop! Four shots. It sound-ed like a cap gun," Louis McPhee, the manager of a car wash across the street, explained to a *Boston Globe* reporter. As Andrade lay bleeding, still clutching his baby girl, Bishop sped away. A passerby scooped up the 10-month-old, splattered with her father's blood but miraculously unharmed, and held the crying child until police and paramedics arrived.

Witnesses to the shooting say they saw Bishop, 60, a grandfather, shoot Andrade four times in the head and torso before leaving the scene. He was later arrested at his home after an eyewitness reported his license plate number to police. When authorities arrived at his residence, he immediately admitted his involvement in the incident.

Andrade died later in hospital. His girlfriend spoke through an interpreter to *Boston Globe* reporters. Visibly shaken, she was with friends and family the following day, comforting her wide-eyed child as the media descended on their home. Annabella Fernandez said her boyfriend had been a hard-working man. Befuddled and shocked, she expressed dismay that her little girl had been exposed to such extreme violence at such a tender age.

"She has no father," said Manuel Mendes, 50, one of Andrade's cousins. "Now the family is her father. She will be taken care of."

In many ways, Andrade was living the American dream—working hard and pursuing big goals for himself and his young family. His father, Artur, was baffled by his son's violent end. Speaking to reporters, he expressed doubt that his son would have been capable of the sort of fury Bishop claims to have experienced. "He was a friendly person. He had a lot of friends. I don't know why this happened."

Bishop was arrested and charged with murder. He later told police that he had feared the younger man had taken down his license plate number in order to exact revenge later. He also claimed his wife was distressed by the earlier incident and that he had acted to protect her.

Bishop's neighbors described him as a friendly but quiet man who diligently tended his garden and chatted amiably with area residents. "He was the perfect neighbor," Joe Denson told the *Boston Globe*.

Bishop appeared pale and stricken during his arraignment, at which he pleaded not guilty to the murder charge. His attorney, Kevin Reddington, argued in court on August 3, 2005, that Andrade had provoked Bishop. The gaunt defendant stood silently in his prison uniform and shackles during the proceedings. According to local media, Bishop has emphysema and requires two tanks of oxygen daily to assist his breathing. He was also taking two kinds of medication for depression. It is possible that Bishop's use of anti-depressants could be used in court to argue the man wasn't in a healthy mental state and that his depression caused him to react as violently as he did.

Reddington was quoted in an Associated

Press article as saying: "We have a homicide that resulted from a circumstance where somebody picked a fight with an individual who obviously exploded." But district attorney Timothy Cruz was not convinced Bishop was as frightened as he claimed. "There was a verbal altercation, after which time the accused, who had a gun, left the scene and returned with a weapon. He then, in cold blood, shot an unarmed man, as he held his child at 8 o'clock in the morning. This is a matter of public record." In a telephone interview, Cruz went on to say his office intends to seek the maximum penalty for Bishop, life in prison. Bishop is being held without bail, in keeping with Massachusetts law. The trial is expected to take place this year.

Everyday people, extraordinary events

In March 2005, when Tampa citizen Michelle Fernandez found herself being aggressively chased by another motorist, the Florida woman's first thoughts were for her 10-year-old son and three-year-old daughter in the back seat of her green Ford Expedition.

The family was headed to a local baseball field when, for no apparent reason, a black Nissan cut across her path, its driver clearly in a rage. Fernandez had no way of knowing that a simple little bumper sticker was fuelling the hostility of her aggressor. Even though she is a registered Democrat, Fernandez had a "Bush/Cheney '04" sticker on the rear of her vehicle. Its pro-Bush message struck a nerve with 31-year-old Nathan Alan Winkler, a zealous Democrat who steadfastly opposed the war in Iraq.

Winkler pulled alongside Fernandez, honking his horn to draw attention to a sheet of white paper he was waving. The letter-sized sign read: "Never Forget Bush's Illegal Oil War Murdered Thousands in Iraq."

Fernandez recounted the bizarre ordeal to reporters from the *St. Petersburg Times*. "At first I didn't know why he was screaming at me," she said, "but then it clicked." Thinking quickly, the frightened mother dialed 911 on her cell phone. While continuing to drive, she provided a moment-by-moment account of her ordeal.

"I was just almost run off the road by a man," she told the dispatcher. "He just ran me off because I have a Bush bumper sticker on my car."

Winkler continually veered his vehicle into the frightened woman's path. As Fernandez disobeyed traffic signs, weaving in and out of traffic to escape from the enraged Winkler, her tone of voice became more urgent. "Oh, now he's following me! I don't know what to do!" She told the 911 dispatcher: "I'm shaking like a leaf."

The dispatcher was able to hear everything Fernandez said, and her remarks told of a confusing and dangerous situation. Winkler's behavior was impossible to predict. At one point, he forced Fernandez to stop her vehicle. "Look, he just pulled over next to me. He's stopping the car. It's ridiculous, this man! Look, he's running

ROAD RAGE CASE STUDIES

after my car." And then, "Oh, my goodness, he's a fanatic. He's in the middle of the street! Now he's following me. He's trying to hurt us. Look at this, what a moron! Look at him! Idiot!"

Eventually, however, Fernandez was able to get away from Winkler. In spite of having to concentrate on her evasive maneuvers, she had been able to make note of the other vehicle's license plate number. She immediately filed a police report in person.

Officials later praised Fernandez, complimenting her for the way she had handled the potentially volatile situation. Joe Durkin, a Tampa Bay police spokesperson, said: "She did all the right things. She showed remarkable poise. She didn't engage him, she called us."

Police arrived at Winkler's home within an hour of the incident. After finding the antiwar sign in his car, they arrested him without incident and booked him into the county jail on one count of aggravated stalking, a third-degree felony punishable by up to five years in prison.

Public relations officer Durkin joked with reporters. "I guess this was a disgruntled Democrat," he said. "Maybe he has that sign with him so he's prepared any time he comes up against a Republican." But, on a more serious note, he pointed out the dangers inherent in Winkler's actions. "This could have been tragic, for her and for her children, and for other people on the road as this was going on."

"I respect [Winkler] for having his beliefs, and for feeling so strongly," Fernandez said later that night, her voice still shaking. "But here he is protesting the war and lost lives, and yet he is going to put me and my children in danger? This man has a serious problem."

Janee Murphy, chairwoman of Hillsborough's Democratic Executive Committee, emphatically distanced her political party from Winkler's actions, telling reporters she couldn't quite grasp why someone would become so agitated. "It's just sad, no matter what your political beliefs are," she said. "We don't need people fighting with each other at home when we have so much going on in the Middle East."

Winkler's father, John Winkler, 59, didn't know about the incident until a *St. Petersburg Times* reporter called him. "That is so not like Nathan," he said. "I know that he is very anti-Bush, but I don't see him doing anything like that. He's certainly not aggressive. He's the least aggressive person I know."

An everyday family outing turned into a terrifying journey for Michelle Fernandez and her children. Fortunately, nobody was killed in their brush with Winkler, but the irrational behavior of their assailant brought them face-to-face with the reality of road rage, where aggression, ignorance, and plain bad manners can turn a highway into a battle zone.

The most hated man in America

On a bleak day in February 2000, California resident Sara McBurnett was driving near the San Jose airport, with her 10-year-old bichon frise dog, Leo, riding shotgun. She had no idea that what was about to happen would thrust her into the media spotlight and spark a wave of outrage across the country. What should have been a minor fender-bender, resulting in an exchange of phone numbers, was about to escalate into a highly publicized case of road rage.

That day, while driving on one of the busiest freeways in the United States, Andrew Douglas Burnett, a PacBell repairman with a history of violent outbursts, cut abruptly in front of McBurnett's vehicle. McBurnett couldn't brake in time and she struck the back of Burnett's black SUV. Both drivers pulled their vehicles to the side of the road. Shaken, McBurnett waited anxiously in her car for the other driver to react.

After leaping out of his car to inspect the damage, Burnett approached McBurnett's car. Somewhere between the two vehicles, he became visibly enraged. He rapped on McBurnett's window and she rolled it down. Leo jumped onto her lap, wagging his tail in greeting. He was a friendly dog, known for approaching strangers in trust and with confidence.

According to McBurnett's trial testimony, the angry man reached through her open car window, snatched Leo out of her lap, and hurled the fluffy white dog directly into oncoming traffic. Burnett then turned and ran, vaulting back into his SUV. Gunning the engine, he pulled back onto the highway, cut across several lanes of traffic, and disappeared.

McBurnett watched in helpless horror as her dog, running back toward her with wild, frightened eyes, was struck by a car.

She bolted out of her car and ran into oncoming traffic with little regard for her own safety to retrieve her beloved pet. Scooping up the tiny dog, she rushed him to a nearby veterinarian as quickly as possible, but it was too late. Leo died on the operating table.

The incident sparked an outpouring of support from around the world and a reward was offered for information on Burnett's whereabouts.

Donations surged to well over $120,000 as well wishers opened their checkbooks. McBurnett appeared on the *Oprah Winfrey Show*, pleading for anyone who had seen her dog's killer to notify police. Web sites sprang up with offers of emotional support for the young woman, and an artist's sketch of Burnett was posted on the Internet. Eventually, an anonymous tip led police to the former telephone repairman. He was charged under animal cruelty laws and arrested without incident.

Burnett's defense attorney, Marc Garcia, said it was virtually impossible for his client to get a fair trial. "The deck was stacked against him from Day 1," he told Associated Press reporters. During the trial, Burnett was painted as a subhuman character, with a history of lying to authorities and stealing tools from his former employer, Pacific Bell.

The case was full of odd revelations, including a claim by Burnett that he had once swerved to avoid hitting a deer, rolled his van down an embankment, and then limped all the way home on foot. However, attempts to show Burnett as a defender of animals didn't ring true to the judge or the jury.

Burnett's fiancée, Jackie Figgins, spoke up for her husband-to-be, describing him as a good man who would never intentionally hurt anyone or anything, including pets. She described him as "loving" and "very sweet," and insisted he would do anything for anyone. She also claimed he was not the kind of person the prosecution had depicted in court. "He feels very bad for Sara McBurnett, because the dog died," Figgins said.

But Figgins's testimony did nothing to explain her fiancé's outrageous actions. According to attorney Garcia, Burnett claimed he had instinctively grabbed the dog because Leo had bit him on the hand. Prosecutor Troy Benson responded: "Andrew Burnett is the only person in the whole world who would think this was reasonable."

The jury also heard tapes of recorded telephone conversations in which Burnett had spoken from jail with his mother and his fiancée. On one tape, Burnett and Figgins discussed selling their story to the media for $250,000 and going on a talk show to have a "dog-kicking contest." These recorded conversations directly contradicted Figgins's claim that Burnett felt kindly towards animals, and did little to increase the likelihood of a sympathetic response from the jury.

On June 19, 2001, Burnett was found guilty of felony animal cruelty and sentenced to the maximum of three years behind bars. After hearing the guilty verdict, McBurnett hugged her lawyer and the courtroom erupted in applause.

"He killed my baby right in front of me," she told the multitudes of media gathered at the courthouse. "I think Abraham Lincoln said you can judge the heart of a man by his treatment of animals." Photos of Leo, head cocked to one side with huge brown eyes, can still be found on the Internet.

Burnett was freed in 2003, but in February of that year, while he was still in prison, he filed a $1-million lawsuit against San Jose's *Mercury News* and Sara McBurnett. He cited a cluster of post-traumatic stress disorder symptoms, including "mental pain and anguish, humiliation, fright and shock, and mortification." He included a request, ultimately denied by the judge, to have his legal costs waived. When informed of the lawsuit, McBurnett said Burnett's attorney "must be a weasel."

Hammer attack in New Zealand

Toma Lauaki, a 35-year-old native of Auckland, New Zealand's capital, had a lot on his mind as he pulled out from a car park onto a stretch of highway outside the city in August 2005. His wife, who was in the passenger seat beside him, had been ill for some time. His concern for her weighed heavily on his mind—so much so, that he didn't realize he'd cut off another driver.

The first he knew about it was when a large rig pulled up behind him. Initially, he paid no attention to the much larger truck until he heard repetitive honking. In a matter of moments, the other truck was weaving around behind him and driving aggressively. Eventually, the truck forced Lauaki's smaller vehicle to the curb. This proved too much for Lauaki to take, and he snapped.

A nearby security camera recorded the entire incident. Lauaki jumped out of his van, hammer in hand, and approached the rig. Reaching up, he hauled driver Barry Fletcher out of the cab. The smaller of the two men, Fletcher fell six feet (2 m) to the pavement, snapping his wrist. Still in a rage, Lauaki began to bludgeon Fletcher as he lay splayed on the ground. The hammer's long claw pierced Fletcher's leg, goring him to the bone.

"He kept yelling, 'Apologize! Apologize!'" recalls Fletcher. "And I kept saying, 'I'm sorry! I don't know what I've done!'" He later described Lauaki's eyes as "black holes of fury," recalling that he was certain the other man was lining up his weapon for a final, deadly blow to Fletcher's head. The arrival of other motorists stopped the attack before Lauaki could deliver any more hits to the helpless man lying on the road. "I have no doubt he was trying to kill me," Fletcher told the Associated Press from his hospital bed shortly after the attack.

Frank Hogan, Lauaki's lawyer, argued that Fletcher was driving in an unsafe manner and had forced his client into a dangerous situation. Hogan also noted Fletcher's truck was much larger than Lauaki's, which his client had found intimidating.

Judge Jane Lovell-Smith told Lauaki the minimum sentence for his crime was seven years in prison, but she took into account his early guilty plea, the fact he was under severe emotional stress at the time due to his wife's illness, and his apparently genuine remorse. She also took into account testimony that indicated Fletcher's driving had been erratic. Before passing sentence, she commented, "What you did, Mr. Lauaki, was to take the law into your own hands, which cannot be condoned in our society." Ultimately, for Lauaki's vicious assault on Fletcher, Judge Lovell-Smith sentenced the hammer-wielding attacker to five years in jail.

As long ago as 1997, New Zealand's then-transport minister Jenny Shipley had urged legislators to consider both community action and media efforts to combat road rage. However, incidents like the one between Lauaki and Fletcher still occur, much to the unease of drivers throughout that nation.

The stakes get higher

On November 8, 2005, a gravel pit worker named Jason Reynolds was driving on a busy stretch of the E-470 freeway outside of Denver, Colorado. The 32-year-old was no stranger to the law. Weeks earlier, he had nearly rammed an unmarked police car shortly before being pulled over for reckless driving. The arresting officer had detected marijuana on Reynolds's breath. Earlier in the year, Reynolds had been charged with ramming the back of another vehicle in a road-rage incident. In fact, in an 18-month period, the Colorado state patrol had received three road-rage-related complaints about Reynolds from nervous drivers who had had contact with him. He had accumulated 13 traffic offenses within a decade, and his demeanor with other drivers had changed from impatience to aggression.

On this fateful day, Reynolds was angry at being delayed behind a Toyota 4-Runner on the busy freeway. Fifty-year-old Kelvin Norman, the driver of the Toyota, was obeying the speed limit. He refused to speed up and let Jason Reynolds pass. Reynolds tailgated Norman for a while, until his impatience got the better of him. He overtook the Toyota, then swerved directly in front of Norman and slammed on his brakes. Norman veered to the left, but collided with Reynolds's Jeep Wrangler. The impact launched his 4-Runner over the divider into oncoming traffic. The Toyota flipped in mid-air and landed on top of a Ford Explorer. Norman was explosively ejected from the cabin of his vehicle, even though he was wearing a seatbelt. He died instantly. Greg Boss, the 35-year-old driver of the Explorer, also died when he was decapitated and dismembered.

Reynolds, whose recklessness was the cause of the mayhem, was completely unharmed. Even though he was standing just a few hundred feet (about 100 m) from the carnage, witnesses say he was unmoved. A tow-truck driver later told the court that Reynolds showed no remorse for what happened, describing him as "almost heartless."

Reynolds was initially charged with two counts of first-degree murder. At his first court appearance, district attorney Carol Chambers added more charges to the indictment, including driving under the influence of drugs and reckless driving. Judge Marilyn Antrim denied bail for Reynolds. "I feel the defendant did not intend to cause the deaths of these two people specifically, but he knowingly engaged in conduct that could result in the death of another," she told the court at his March 10, 2006 arraignment.

His trial is scheduled for July 24, 2006. If found guilty of first-degree murder, Reynolds faces life in prison, possibly even the death penalty. The case has far-reaching implications. It could set a precedent for other jurisdictions to try road-rage incidents that result in death as murder, rather than as vehicular homicide, which carries a lighter sentence.

Michael Zizzi, a PhD candidate at the University of Colorado at Boulder, says the big tragedy is that society let Norman down by not teaching him the behavioral language that may have saved him. Zizzi suggests that Norman may have slowed down to show his displeasure with Reynolds's tailgating. Had he known the potential for the situation to explode, he could have moved into the right lane and let the agitated driver pass. If Norman had been taught to avoid conflict, tragedy might have been avoided.

The busy software engineer

Running late for work is one of the most commonly cited explanations for frustration and anger on our roads. When Anna Gitlin, a software engineer on her way to work south of Boston, Massachusetts, came across a roadblock erected after a fatal crash, she refused to let it stop her from getting to her job on time. She viewed the roadblock with disdain, and then verbally abused the officers at the scene. "I don't care who (expletive) died. I'm more important," Gitlin yelled.

When Officer Steven Shalno asked Gitlin for her license and registration, she refused to give them to him. As he reached into her car, she snapped the window shut on his arm and started to drive away, hurling him to the ground. The

ROAD RAGE CASE STUDIES

officer suffered injuries to his legs and hip from the impact.

A truck driver who witnessed the incident pulled his rig across the road to prevent Gitlin from getting away. She was arrested at the scene. The date was June 24, 2003.

Gitlin admitted to two counts of assault and battery with a dangerous weapon—her car, as well as two counts of assault and battery on a police officer, driving negligently, and disorderly conduct.

Judge Paul Chernoff sentenced Gitlin to two years in the county jail, but he suspended the sentence and placed her on probation for five years. The first year of probation must be served under home confinement; Gitlin may leave the house only from 6 a.m. to 6 p.m., to attend her job. If she violates her probation, she could be required to serve the jail sentence. Gitlin must complete 500 hours of community service and pay a fine of $5,000, the maximum allowed for assault and battery on a police officer. She was also ordered to write a letter of apology to the officer, who missed several months of work while recovering from his injuries.

Murder on the bus

The red double-decker buses of London, England, have long been a symbol of the British capital. Tourists and locals alike clamber to the upper levels for stellar views of the dynamic city. However, at midnight on March 28, 2005, even the crush of the double-deckers or the equally famous London Tube provided safer modes of transport than did London's streets.

At a busy intersection in central London, Peter Kelly's red car came too close to three men who were crossing the road. He nearly ran one of them over. The three men jeered at him. Kelly drove halfway up the block and stopped his car. Wielding a large metal chain, he began chasing the pedestrians on foot.

He chased them through the streets of London until they leapt onto a bus, hoping to avoid his anger. By then, Kelly had exchanged the metal chain for a knife and was in a raging fury. He jumped onto the bus and approached one of the men with a nine-inch (23 cm) blade in his hand. "Do you want to die?" he screamed.

Kelly didn't appear deterred by, or even aware of, the presence of other people, and didn't hesitate as he stabbed the man. He brazenly plunged his knife upward into the chest of Bartosz Dlugowszewski, killing him. As the bus passengers looked on in horror, he pulled the blade out of the man's heart and calmly walked off the bus and ran down a nearby street. According to the story in the *South London Press*, he then walked to his grandmother's house and drank a bottle of whiskey.

As prosecutor Michael Worsley later told the court, being taunted by the three men had set Kelly off. Eyewitnesses to the attack described Kelly as "howling mad," and video footage shows him in a rage, teeth bared, ready to attack. Judge Geoffrey Rivlin sentenced Kelly to life imprisonment for Dlugowszewski's murder, with a minimum of 12 years behind bars before parole could be considered.

CHAPTER 4

Road Rage Around the World

British drivers rank among the most aggressive drivers in the world. Dr. David Lewis, a British psychologist and specialist in stress reduction, notes that drivers in the United Kingdom today are much less courteous to one another than they used to be. He believes that the prevailing push toward success and excess in western society is partially to blame for the Brits' self-absorbed approach to driving.

Current attitudes celebrate wealth and put little stock in down time. People are in a tremendous rush to beat the clock and arrive on time and, because of this, they lose patience easily. In addition, he speculates, they've lost faith in their fellow drivers and view them as the enemy.

Lewis cites an incident that received some media attention in London in 2004. According to Lewis, two men got into a brawl following a motoring disagreement in the streets of the British city. It's no longer an uncommon sight in the United Kingdom to see two people duke it out on the streets over a traffic dispute. But, in this case, it came to light that one man was a rabbi, and the other a Buddhist priest. It would appear no one is immune to fury behind the wheel.

* * *

In the bustling city of Belgrade, Serbia, traffic snarls are an accepted part of everyday life. For most citizens of the embattled country, road woes are low on their list of priorities. However, when a security guard at the U.S. embassy took issue with the way Serbian leader Boris Tadic's motorcade was progressing, he slammed his vehicle into one of the cars to indicate his frustration.

Local media rushed to call it an assassination attempt, but it was later discovered to be a case of road rage. Officials said the driver, Miroslav Cimpl, was agitated by the slow pace at which President Tadic's vehicles were being driven through the Belgrade traffic.

* * *

Gun legislation often comes up as a connected topic when armed road-rage incidents end in tragedy. In April 2002, in the Paris suburb of Vannes, a man with a history of gun violence ran a red light and collided with another vehicle. The youths whose vehicle had been struck gave chase, but they soon became the pursued when Jean-Charles Denis turned toward them brandishing a Kalashnikov rifle. The young men fled to a nearby police station, but even there, there was no sanctuary as Jean-Charles Denis, a 48-year-old horse breeder, showered the station with bullets. When the dust settled, one police officer, Regis Ryckebusch, was dead.

Denis was ultimately shot in the shoulder by a police officer. At that point, Denis, a member of the Brittany Liberation Front with a record of violent behavior, was arrested and taken into custody. At the time of his arrest, he was carrying a pistol and a knife, as well as the Kalashnikov rifle.

The case sparked a wave of outrage in France and many questioned how a man with such a violent history was allowed access to an assault rifle. In an interview with a radio station, then-prime minister Lionel Jospin blamed his conservative political opponents for blocking an earlier attempt to tighten gun laws. He added: "As far as I am concerned, I am totally ready for this legislation to be tougher and harder still."

Road rage is violent enough all by itself, but the combination of road rage and guns is a deadly one.

* * *

In Australia, roads appear to have become safer in recent decades. The Australian Bureau of Transport Safety says the number of road fatalities declined from a high of 30 fatalities per 100,000 people in 1970 to just less than 10 per 100,000 in 1997. The overall number of fatalities declined from 3,798 in 1970 to 1,764 in 1997, despite the rapid growth in the number of cars on the road (4.8 million in 1970 versus 11.4 million in 1997).

However, beginning in 1997, the fatality rate stopped declining and, in fact, had risen to 1,818 deaths in 2000. Despite measures, such as banning the use of cell phones while driving, it would appear the level of frustration "down under" is just as high as elsewhere in the world.

Painting a bleak picture of driver courtesy, an Australian insurance firm found that among drivers surveyed, nearly half admitted to making rude hand gestures or shouting at other motorists whom they perceived as being in the wrong. According to that same study, most drivers didn't consider their own behavior as antisocial or misguided.

The number of drivers who admitted to being so frustrated that they had tailgated another car while flashing their lights had almost tripled, from five percent in 1996 to 14 percent in 2005.

* * *

In Japan, a prison created just for delinquent and angry drivers has had a profound impact. The 420-bed Ichihara prison, built in 1969, punishes aggressive and dangerous drivers. Ichihara's methods seem harsh by North American standards. The discipline includes a dress code with crew cuts and pressed uniforms, silence during meals, and isolation—where inmates are expected to meditate on their shortcomings—for those who break the rules. Inmates are also expected to make restitution and feel remorse for their crimes.

Some Japanese believe Ichihara is still too lenient, but the prison's approach seems to be effective. Only 7.7 percent of prisoners return to the facility after their first incarceration.

CHAPTER 5

Celebrities and Road Rage

No one is immune to the feelings of frustration and aggression that can lead to road rage. Celebrities are particularly at risk, some would argue, because of their relentless pursuit by paparazzi photographers and news reporters. Already under the media microscope, celebrities are often hauled before a judge after losing their cool behind the wheel.

The Juice is loose

O.J. Simpson faced legal scrutiny after one such altercation in Miami, Florida, on December 4, 2000.

The defendant in one of the most infamous criminal trials in U.S. history, Simpson became a household name in the late 1990s. The media circus surrounding his double murder trial was unprecedented. The former football star was a nightly fixture on television for close to nine months as the world watched his criminal trial for the 1994 murder of his ex-wife, Nicole Brown Simpson, and her friend, Ronald Goldman. He was found not guilty. But in 1997, in a lawsuit filed by Goldman's family in civil court—where standards of proof are lower—he was found to be liable for Goldman's death and fined $8.5 million. The civil court also declared him to have committed battery against Nicole, even though the Brown family had not filed a suit or sought damages.

In October 2001, O.J. was in the news again

when a jury found him not guilty of battery and auto burglary charges stemming from a road-rage incident in early December 2000. Had he been found guilty, he would have faced a maximum of 16 years behind bars.

The road-rage incident arose when Simpson's neighbor, Jeffrey Pattinson, accused Simpson of attacking him after a verbal exchange on a Miami side street. According to *Court TV* transcripts of the trial, Pattinson, 55, began tailing Simpson after he saw the former football star run a stop sign in his black Lincoln Navigator, nearly causing an accident. He told prosecutor Abbe Rifkin that Simpson appeared enraged and was acting like a "madman." He also claimed Simpson said, "So I ran the damn stop sign. What are you going to do, kill me and my kids?" Simpson then allegedly reached into Pattinson's vehicle and pulled the sunglasses off his face, not breaking off his attack until he heard his daughter calling to him from the Navigator, saying, "No, Daddy.

No, Daddy. No!"

Simpson, meanwhile, claimed that Pattinson had honked at him repeatedly, flashed his high-beam headlights, and followed him. Simpson also claimed that Pattinson had bolted from his vehicle, screaming and cursing—a direct contradiction of Pattinson's testimony that Simpson assaulted him while he was still in his vehicle.

In keeping with his infamous, often colorful image, Simpson joked with lawyers while testifying. The jury believed Simpson, and he was found not guilty.

> **PROSECUTING CELEBRITIES**
>
> "The initial hurdle in prosecuting celebrities, from the prosecutor's point of view, is to ensure that [you] are not treating the celebrity any differently than [you] would any other person committing the same crime in similar circumstances. In presenting the crime to the jury, one has to be mindful that the jury might be more sympathetic, or less sympathetic, to the celebrity because of who they are, and the prosecutor has to address that in [his/her] opening and/or closing statements."
>
> *Doug Gansler for Court TV, Courttv.com*

Mike Tyson can't cage his rage

Once one of the most celebrated boxers in the world, former world heavyweight champion Mike Tyson has also served hard prison time. In the early 1990s, he was jailed for three years for the alleged rape of Desiree Washington, a contestant in the Miss Black America pageant, marking the beginning of the decline of Mike Tyson.

His infamous 1997 fight against Evander Holyfield for the World Boxing Association title forever tainted Tyson's reputation. Images of him biting the other boxer's ear (which he did on two occasions during the fight) were splashed across the front pages of newspapers worldwide. Tyson was banned from boxing for one year and fined $3 million. His mental state became fodder for jokes and the man known as "Iron Mike" faced a bleak future.

Despite his extreme behavior, subsequent psychiatric evaluations proved Tyson to be of sound mind and he was reissued a boxing license by the Nevada Athletic Commission in

CELEBRITIES AND ROAD RAGE

1999. In January of that year, Tyson fought François Botha, and while Botha initially controlled the fight, Tyson landed a straight right hand in the fifth round that knocked out Botha. The fight was tainted with scandal and Tyson was accused of trying to break the other man's arm. Still, he seemed to be getting his life on track. He had married a doctor, Monika Steele, and was volunteering at a homeless shelter.

As the boxing world waited with bated breath for his second fight, yet another scandal rocked their world. Tyson was back in court—this time, charged with assaulting two people after a car accident on August 31, 1998.

It's no secret that Iron Mike has a temper; it's part of what made him a prizefighter. However, he has difficulty controlling his rage outside the boxing ring. Doctors had prescribed antidepressants to combat the feelings of frustration he felt after slogging through seemingly endless legal battles. So, when he leapt out of his wife's Mercedes after a minor fender-bender with all his warrior instincts kicking in, the fallout was immediate and public. Two other cars were involved in the incident. Tyson bellowed threats to the other drivers. One quickly rolled up his window and locked his door, but Tyson's bodyguard lured the man out of his car. He was rewarded with a kick to the groin. The other driver was punched in the face.

Abmielec Saucedo and Richard Hardick subsequently indicated that they did not believe Tyson should be sent to jail, but that didn't stop prosecutors from pressing charges. Later, both men stated they didn't feel the altercation warranted a trial. Ultimately, both accepted large payouts from Tyson.

But Judge Stephen Johnson said the boxer had demonstrated "potentially lethal road rage." On February 5, 1999, Tyson was sentenced to a year's imprisonment, fined $5,000, and ordered to perform 200 hours of community service for the assault. He served nine months of that sentence.

Tyson quit boxing in June 2005 after a series of losses, but this didn't calm his temper. In March 2006, Tyson hit the headlines again. As his motorcade made its way along a highway near Fort Lauderdale, Florida, the slow progress of traffic set off the brawny boxer. After asking his chauffeur to pull onto the shoulder, he leapt out of his limo and began pacing back and forth alongside the busy freeway. Isadore Bolton, a driver and personal assistant to promoter Don King, left his convoy vehicle to check on Tyson.

Rather than thank Bolton for his concern, Tyson delivered two heavyweight punches to the face. Bolton fell to the ground in agony, but Tyson's rage was unabated. Onlookers watched in horror as Tyson proceeded to bite a large chunk out of Bolton's leg.

The case did not go to trial; Tyson paid $275,000 to Bolton but did not admit liability in the incident.

The linebacker versus the city clerk

Stephen Towle still holds the single-season tackle record for the Miami Dolphins. The six-foot-three 52-year-old hasn't played football in years and until recently, was living a quiet life in Lee's Summit, Kansas.

In September 2005, Rudy Babbitt, a 49-year-old retired city clerk, was driving along the highway outside Independence, Missouri, with his 15-year-old son, William. His health wasn't very good and he was taking blood thinners after a recent heart attack.

The first time the two drivers became aware of each other was when they met on highways 291 and 40. Towle cut in front of Babbitt, forcing him to slam on his brakes. Babbitt's concern for his son motivated him to get out of his car to confront the other driver. He could not have known he would be facing 300 pounds of former National Football League player. After a heated exchange, Towle struck Babbitt several times in the head. The smaller man was no match for him and he crumpled under the force of the blows.

Babbitt's head smacked against the concrete as he fell to the ground and the force of the trauma caused severe brain hemorrhaging. Doctors operated for hours to stop the bleeding and Babbitt was in intensive care for weeks. His family thought he wasn't going to survive. Even today, after numerous surgeries, Babbitt is still limited in his mobility and speech and lives with his mother.

Towle was arrested and charged with second-degree assault. The judge gave him a suspended sentence, ordered five years' probation, and awarded restitution of $125,000 to Babbittt, most of which went to pay his legal fees. Towle was also ordered to take anger-management classes.

Babbittt's mother was outraged at what she deemed an unjust sentence. "He'll never be the same. We'll never have him back, and this guy is going to walk free. It's not justice," she said after the sentence was handed down.

The defense attorney said that Towle was "sorry the circumstance occurred."

The NRA lobbyist's son

Americans have a long-standing love-hate relationship with guns. Many argue that the right to bear arms is central to their personal freedom, while others claim that guns are at the root of all violence in the United States.

Therefore, it's not surprising that gun lobbyists and anti-gun lobbyists abound in the halls of Washington. Among the pro-gun lobbyists is the chairman of the American Conservative Union, David Keene. He has campaigned vigorously for the rights of hunters and gun owners. He fought passionately against the airlines that wanted to stop carrying hunting weapons to Africa. Keene is the face for gun owner's rights in the United States. Recently, he was re-elected to the National Rifle Association's board of directors, a group he enthusiastically defends.

So when his son, David Michael Keene, was thrust into the media spotlight after he erupted in his own case of road rage, the elder Keene and his wife, Diana Carr, pleaded for mercy from the media. It appears to have been effective. There has been little media coverage of the crime.

On December 1, 2002, the 21-year-old Keene was driving his BMW on the George Washington Parkway in Washington, DC, when he engaged in a verbal altercation with a man named Homayoon Zaiee. The exchange escalated and Keene fired his .40-caliber weapon at the other man's Mercedes as they both sped along. In a stroke of luck, the bullet lodged in the driver's seat, inches away from Zaiee's head, and he drove away from the shooting unharmed.

Zaiee then called police and gave them the license plate number of the car from which the shots were fired. Keene was arrested at his home and appeared in court on December 5, 2002.

Concern for his image prompted the elder Keene to release the following statement shortly after his son's arrest: "The actions of my adult son were not and are not related in any way to my political beliefs or work and it would be unfair of anyone to insinuate that such a connection exists."

A grand jury indicted Keene on three counts: assault with a dangerous weapon; using, brandishing, and discharging a firearm during a crime of violence; and making a false statement in his application for a gun permit. The fresh-faced but troubled young man has a long history of mental health problems. At the time of his arrest, Keene Jr. was the director of online communications for the American Conservative Union. He immediately resigned from his position.

"He's had a continuing problem with impulse control and an exaggerated belief that he was in more danger than he was in at times, causing him to respond in a way that was more excessive or out of line with what was going on," Keene's mother, Diana Carr, told reporters outside the U.S. District Court in Alexandria shortly after her son's arrest.

She also noted Keene was institutionalized seven times between the ages of eight and 13.

Due to his history of mental health problems, Keene had falsified his firearm application. His fiancée later told reporters they were en route to a firing range and that the gun misfired.

Judge Leonie M. Brinkena wasn't swayed by the defendant's version of events and sentenced him to the maximum under Virginia law—10 years behind bars.

In February 2006, *New Scientist* magazine reported that those who own guns are most likely to become angry enough to engage in road rage. A survey of 2,400 drivers carried out by David Hemenway and his colleagues at the Harvard School of Public Health shows that motorists who carry guns in their cars are far more likely to indulge in road rage than motorists who travel without guns. Some 23 percent of gun-toting drivers admitted to making rude gestures, compared with 16 percent of those who did not carry guns. Perhaps having ready access to a weapon encourages bravado and reckless behavior.

Yet, in some states it is easier than ever to own a gun and carry it in a car. In the past two decades, 23 states have eased restrictions on carrying guns, says researcher Mary Vriniotis.

The lethal mix of rage and guns has yet to provoke U.S. lawmakers into providing more stringent legislation, and drivers never know who has a pistol stored in their glove compartment until it's too late.

CHAPTER 6

Efforts to Reduce Road Rage

In 1997, the United States Congress created a special committee to gain a better understanding of the contributing factors in road rage. Calling witnesses from among law enforcement personnel, health practitioners, and concerned citizens, the panel's recommendations are being implemented across a wide range of agencies. But it's a tricky business. As Patrick Bedard wrote in *Car and Driver,* "How do you criminalize impatience?"

Most states in the United States have enacted laws aimed at reckless driving, which includes a broad scope of behaviors. Other states have enacted laws specifically targeting aggressive drivers (which implies malice). To date (2006), 10 states have either enacted aggressive driving legislation or have updated existing reckless driving statutes to include aggressive driving. Aggressive driving laws typically stipulate that a driver must be observed demonstrating more than one aggressive behavior. An additional 17 states introduced aggressive driving bills between 1999 and 2003: Connecticut, Hawaii, Illinois, Kansas, Louisiana, Massachusetts, Michigan, Missouri, New Hampshire, New York, North Carolina, Oklahoma, Pennsylvania, South Carolina, Tennessee, Texas, and Washington (which passed Bill 5160 in January 2006).

Twenty-four states have public education campaigns to illustrate the dangers of aggressive driving and to provide safety tips. These initiatives usually publicize enforcement efforts or provide phone numbers for reporting dangerous drivers.

Other initiatives offer legislation with rigorous enforcement, media demonizing of aggressive driving, public education, and intervention classes for repeat offenders, in a combined approach to aggressive driving. One such example is the "Smooth Operator" law enforcement program developed by the National Highway Traffic Safety Administration, which specifically targets aggressive driving. Such anger-management programs remain a viable option for drivers who can't

> **SMOOTH OPERATOR INITIATVE**
>
> The Smooth Operator program was started in 1997 to provide education, information, and solutions for the problem of aggressive driving. The program is a partnership among Maryland, Virginia, and Washington, DC, law enforcement agencies, trauma experts, government officials, and other professionals, who are working together to educate motorists about the risks involved with aggressive driving, and to stigmatize aggressive driving behavior.

control their tempers. Other methods of addressing the problem utilize technological advances such as photo radar.

Some states are lagging behind. In Florida, the senate and the house passed a sweeping bill that would see tougher penalties for aggressive driving, tailgating, and speeding. However, Florida Governor Jeb Bush felt it would discourage tourism, and vetoed it in May 2005.

In New York, state police introduced road-rage vans with video equipment in the late 1990s. Working with marked trooper cars during aggressive driving enforcement campaigns, the vans record aggressive driving incidents and communicate them to the trooper cars, which then pull over the ragers. The New York State police define an aggressive driver as one who operates a motor vehicle in a selfish, bold, or pushy manner, without regard for the rights or safety of others.

In addition, "slick roof" trooper cars are being used in New York's campaign to stem the tide of aggressive driving. Equipped with video cameras to record aggressive drivers, the strobe lights of these low-profile marked cars are located in the headlights, tail lamps, and turn signals. The enforcement efforts complement a statewide education campaign sponsored by the governor's Traffic Safety Commission. Its slogan is: "Steer clear of aggressive driving. Getting there shouldn't be half the battle."

Curbing aggressive driving through driver education has proved a success in the state of Virginia. Virginia law requires that driver education courses be offered through the school system, and that they include instruction on aggressive driving. In 2004, a Virginia bill requiring driver improvement courses for repeat aggressive driving offenders was withdrawn when the Department of Motor Vehicles (DMV) voluntarily implemented the curriculum. The Virginia DMV now offers instruction designed to quell aggressive driving behavior and rehabilitate aggressive drivers. The purpose of the class is to raise students' awareness and teach them how to identify and avoid aggressive drivers.

Another initiative was begun in Miami, where road-rage incidents are commonplace. The thriving metropolis often places in the top five cities for road rage. In 1999, a group of savvy drivers formed Roadrageous, a company that offers a driving safety course created by the American Institute for Public Safety (AIPS) to help address the problem of aggressive driving. The North Miami company—a multimillion-dollar national operation with 40 employees at its headquarters—is the same organization that made traffic school fun with their Improv Traffic Schools, founded by AIPS president Gary Alexander in California in 1985. Using stand-up comedians to illustrate how ludicrous most cases of road rage really are, the company engages drivers in a lighthearted way.

"There are two types of drivers: morons and idiots," Michael Panzeca joked with his captive audience. "Morons in the slow cars ahead, idiots zooming past you.

"Once I saw how this course was affecting my driving, being more aware and less judgmental, I realized it was a good thing we were offering," said Panzeca, who has taught the better driving instruction (BDI) course for four years. "People will do things in a car that they wouldn't normally do because of the sense of anonymity."

"We don't make fun of safety; we make safety fun," says Chris Huffman, CEO of AIPS and a self-confessed aggressive driver. "We believe that Roadrageous will parallel the points of action in what they did to address [driving under the influence] five years ago," Huffman said, adding, "Start at a grass-roots level; enforce it judicially and then educate. ... Acknowledge that at one time or another everyone has demonstrated aggressive driving. Recognize it, witness it, and modify your behavior."

Carbusters.org makes no bones about its solution to road rage: fewer cars on the roads and more sustainable modes of transportation. It works in tandem with Road Peace, a charity set up in 1992 to represent road-crash victims and to draw attention to victims' lack of rights before the law. The non-profit organization initiated a remembrance day for victims of car accidents. Because these accidents are commonplace—3,000 killed and 100,000 injured each day, worldwide—there are not the memorials or monuments that would normally accompany disasters of such proportions. Road Peace documents the experiences of road-crash victims and then uses them to lobby policy makers for stricter laws.

Driving while on the phone

Cell phones are commonly cited as the number one distraction on today's roads, and have led to countless road-rage incidents. Some advocates of a full ban of cell phone use while driving claim the level of distraction caused by the use of cell phones is equivalent to that of driving drunk. A *Prevention Magazine* article noted that 85 percent of cell phone owners do, in fact, talk on their phones while driving.

In the United States, the use of cell phones while driving is legislated on a state-by-state basis. In Washington State, Senator Tracey Eide had been trying for eight years to get the bill, in one form or another, passed. The state senate finally passed Bill 5160 on January 9, 2006. However, the bill stalled when it failed to get a full-house vote. The bill would make it illegal to talk on a hand-held cell phone. The penalty for gabbing and driving was originally set at $101. The prolific use of cell phones now has its own acronym: DWC—driving

DRIVING WHILE CELLPHONING

As of February, 2006, the following states have banned or partially banned the use of cell phones on the road: Connecticut, the District of Columbia, Georgia (school bus drivers only), Maine (adolescents and people who hold learners' permits), New Jersey, New York, and Washington. The remaining states are still debating the laws, have implemented partial bans, or are not pursuing legislation.

while cellphoning.

It is now illegal to drive while using a hand-held phone in many countries around the world, including Australia, Denmark, Egypt, England, France, Germany, Greece, India, Ireland, and Norway. In Ireland, the cost of driving while phoning is high. Fines soar to $380 and prison terms are handed out for third-time offenders. Hands-free use is currently under debate. In Norway, the fines are even steeper—up to $600 per infraction.

In Canada, Newfoundland metes out fines for driving and chatting on cell phones. Since the law was passed there in 2003, none of the other provinces have enacted such sweeping legislation. In 2002, Alberta shot down a proposed law restricting cell phone use while driving. To date, only Ontario and Nova Scotia have proposed legislation that would impose legal limits on the use of hand-held devices while driving. Transport Canada is monitoring how the law is affecting driver safety in Newfoundland.

CHAPTER 7

Tips for Avoiding Road Rage

As a professor at Regis University in Denver, Colorado, Michael Zizzi has studied communication for 20 years. His doctoral thesis focused on driving as a form of communication. We study speeches, writings, books, and movies to determine how they affect us as a society. But, Zizzi claims, no one has looked into the way we drive and how that affects us. He says that when a road-rage incident occurs, it's the end result of a series of interactions on the road. A "conversation" may have begun many minutes before, but no one is aware of the impact of that initial interaction until it swells into an argument.

"That's when we become aware of the people around us. When we're forced into awareness by the angry gesture of another driver, or the sound of a horn, or the flashing of headlights," he said in a telephone interview. "Driving is a conversation. Road rage is what happens when the conversation goes bad."

Zizzi insists that part of the problem is the myopic attitude of so many drivers. They look at what's directly in their line of vision, but no farther. While many people take their daily commutes for granted, or treat them as social occasions, or a time to chat on cell phones or to check their makeup in the rearview mirror, Zizzi said he is acutely aware of what's going on around him. "I drive as though my life depends on it."

He claims to be able to influence the driving patterns of other drivers. For example, if he's in the right lane on a freeway and sees a car farther ahead in the same lane, but speeding, he says if he switches to the left lane to pass, the other driver will instinctively move into the left lane to block his passage.

It goes directly to our need to win, he says. "I need to be ahead of you."

Zizzi also notes that the more money a driver spends on horsepower, the more likely that person is to overreact to a situation and to gun the engine. "I spent $40,000 on this car, so I could be in charge," he says with an incredulous laugh. He also notes that drivers of some vehicles tend to be more aggressive than others. "V-8 jeeps," he says. "They hate to be passed … No one does that to them."

But despite the overwhelming urge to win, those drivers rarely achieve their mission and often end up snarled in traffic, seething with frustration. "Someone who wants to maintain

SORRY!

A SORRY! sign is a simple but effective way to diffuse a potentially lethal road-rage situation. Make this sign, keep it in your car, and use it when you've made a driving error. Here are some guidelines for your SORRY! sign:

- Use plain white paper with solid black print
- Print the word SORRY! in two-inch-high (5 cm) letters, all upper-case
- Use a thick, easy-to-read font for the lettering (for example, **Arial Bold**)
- Surround the word with a blank border at least three-eighths inches (1 cm) wide

If you print it on regular, letter-size printer paper (8½ × 11), you can have it laminated at a business supply store or service center. Use the heaviest lamination available (10-weight, if possible) and leave a border of plastic extending one-quarter of an inch (1 cm) beyond the paper. Be sure to round the edges of the four plastic corners.

Printed in landscape orientation, and with a finished size of approximately 9 x 3½ inches (23 x 9 cm) including lamination, you can fit the word four times on a standard sheet of paper. Hand the spares out to friends!

Source: Awesome Library web site
www.awesomelibrary.org/road-rage.html

power over other drivers isn't going to get very far."

Zizzi says that if those trigger-happy drivers are allowed to pass, they often decompress and the situation doesn't escalate. They think, "I won. It's over. Now to celebrate, I'll slow down." He suggests that if everyone would be more cognizant of the needs and concerns of other drivers, road rage would diminish significantly.

Just as we smile when we're happy or scowl when we're upset, the way we drive is also a form of expression. Zizzi believes that if we pay more attention to our own behavior and that of those around us, we all stand a better chance of avoiding road rage and reaching our destinations unharmed.

His No. 1 tip: "Do not engage in a dialog with

> **DON'T TURN YOUR NOSE UP AT THIS TIP**
>
> Sniff a bit of peppermint or cinnamon to keep you alert while driving. In one study, drivers who were given the peppermint scent recorded significantly lowered levels of fatigue, anxiety, and driver frustration. They also recorded higher alertness ratings.

> ### DEALING WITH AN AGGRESSIVE DRIVER
>
> The New York State police recommend these basic tips for dealing with an aggressive driver:
> - Remain calm.
> - Keep your distance.
> - Do not pass unless you have to.
> - Change lanes once it is safe to do so. (Don't jump lanes without looking.)
> - If you cannot change lanes and an aggressive driver is behind you, stay where you are, maintain the proper speed, and do not respond with hostile gestures.
> - Call 911 (or *911 from a cell phone) to report an aggressive driver or a driver you believe may be impaired.
>
> OF SPECIAL NOTE: If you witness an act of aggressive driving, police cannot issue a ticket simply because you've taken down a license plate number. However, if you travel a particular route on a regular basis and witness aggressive behavior at certain times, state police would be interested in knowing the locations.
>
> *Source: www.nysgtsc.state.ny.us/aggr-ndx.htm*

an angry person, regardless of the perceived slight. That is how the conversation of road rage begins." And, just as conversations require more than one person, an altercation needs both parties for it to escalate. "It takes two, sometimes three or four, to road rage," adds Zizzi

Reduce your chances of being involved in a road rage incident

The National Highway Traffic Safety Administration has provided a useful list of tips to quell rising tempers and ease congestion on busy streets. The following simple tips can help save unnecessary anxiety and possible altercations.

1. Plan ahead If you know that your drive to work averages between 10 and 30 minutes, give yourself 40 minutes. Don't leave late and expect to make up for lost time on the road.

2. Concentrate Give the drive your full attention. Chatting on your cell phone, shaving, eating, drinking, putting on makeup, or reading the newspaper are all distractions and can lead to mistakes.

3. Relax Tune the radio to your favorite radio station. Music can calm your nerves and help you enjoy your time in the car. It is also a means of exerting control over your environment and could prevent feelings of helplessness.

4. Take the road less traveled Map out an alternate route. Even if it looks longer on paper, you may find it is less congested. But don't turn it into a racetrack by speeding.

5. Vary your commuting schedule Talk to your employer about adopting more flexible work hours, starting before the really heavy traffic hits and leaving before the snarls of afternoon rush hour.

6. Telecommute No single technological breakthrough has the potential to alter our work environments as completely as the Internet. Not surprisingly, the trend to working at home or from satellite offices is growing quickly.

TIPS FOR AVOIDING ROAD RAGE

7. Hop on the bus, Gus Most communities offer some form of public transportation. Even though it's less convenient than driving your own car, public transportation can give you some much-needed relief from life behind the wheel. With someone else driving, it can be liberating to enjoy a good read on the way to work.

8. Change jobs This may sound like a drastic step simply to avoid congestion, but a long and difficult commute to and from work every day can seriously diminish your quality of life. Many people are finding that it is not worth it.

9. Just be late Just accept that being late is a part of life and don't sweat it.

Behaviors to avoid

Avoid behaviors such as those listed below, which are likely to provoke aggression.

- **Gestures**—Obscene or offensive gestures irritate other drivers. Be aware that other drivers may misinterpret any physical gesture, even a friendly one.

- **Talking on car phones**—Don't let your phone become a distraction. Car-phone users are perceived as being poor drivers and presenting a traffic hazard. Data show that aggressive drivers are particularly irritated by fender-benders with motorists who were talking on the phone.

- **Displays**—Refrain from displaying bumper stickers, slogans, or vanity license plates that may be considered offensive.

- **Eye contact**—If a motorist tries to pick a fight, do not make eye contact. Get out of the way, without acknowledging the other motorist. If the driver follows you, do not go home. Go to a police station or a location where you can get help and where witnesses will be available.

- **Aggressive tailgating**—Riding the bumper of

TIPS FOR AVOIDING ROAD RAGE

the vehicle in front of you is both annoying to the person being followed and unsafe.

• **Aggressive horn use**—Leaning on the horn to express anger is aggravating.

• **Aggressive headlight use**—Flashing headlights to denote irritation is rude and unsafe.

CHAPTER 8

Looking Ahead— Theories and Suggestions

In a 2005 commentary penned for the *Washington Times*, Robert Charles, former assistant secretary of state for international narcotics and law enforcement, presented some novel ideas on how drivers can quell the rising tide of violence on our roads. Part tongue-in-cheek, part a plea for awareness, Charles's humor-laced ideas make sense.

We should, he noted, engage in road love

rather than road rage. Be nice. He also recommended a series of accessories bound to stir a chuckle in the most irked of drivers. "We could start with a 'Smile, don't curse' line of bumper-stickers, add finger puppets for those prone to be digitally active, install random speed bumps on emotional stretches, and issue a set of window signs that consciously tame tensions—you know, like, 'Have a Nice Rush Hour,' 'Follow Me, I'm Listening to Classical,' 'Whatever Your View, That's Mine,' 'I Brake for Everything,' and 'Who Painted These Lines Anyhow?' "

He stated simply, yet effectively, that drivers need to relearn the art of good manners. "The sky is the limit, and 'road love' could just catch on. We could fight craziness with craziness, get our highways and byways back in some kind of civil shape again ... bring back 'flower-power,' politeness, and the long-defunct friendly wave," he said.

"Or we could do something simpler: slow down and behave better. In the end, that might be easier. And we wouldn't lose Monday through Saturday, have to worry about speed bumps and cameras, end up scattering the dash with finger puppets, or get those uncomfortable stretch marks from over-used smile muscles. We could just do as we used to, and drive in peace. Novel concept, but what do you say?"

Timeline

1984 The term road rage is first coined by a *Los Angeles Times* reporter writing a story about a truck driver who shot another driver who had cut him off. Previously, the term "roid rage" had been used to describe the angry state of steroid users. (Incidentally, a variety of spin-offs—such as desk rage, mall rage, and air rage—have also become part of the general lexicon.)

1994 A throng of road-rage experts appears in various media, and a spate of books is released, all examining the issue through different lenses.

1997 Congress's special surface transportation subcommittee aims to examine the issue of road rage in more precise detail. Calling experts from a wide

ROAD RAGE

range of fields to shed light on the issue, they prepare an exhaustive report and recommend sweeping changes to the laws governing aggressive drivers.

1998 In Toronto, Canada, police receive 500 complaints per week about aggressive drivers.

2001 Road rage becomes such a broadly used term that a Simpson's *Road Rage* video game is released.

2005 Most states in the United States have enacted laws, which itemize a broad range of behaviors, aimed at "reckless driving." However, some states are now beginning to recognize that certain of those driver behaviors are better defined as "aggressive."

What Others Say

"It's really dangerous out there. We take it for granted because we make it home every day."

Rob Campbell, monkeymeter.com

"If you want to insult a man, either tell him he's lousy in bed or tell him he's a lousy driver."

Dr. David Lewis, psychologist

"Anyone who thinks that traffic should flow in his favor, lights should turn green so as not to impede his progress, and other drivers must exercise error-free, perfect judgment is a person suffering from flawed logic. He needs to grow up, develop some impulse control, and stop being so egocentric."

Dr. Phil McGraw, psychologist (in O magazine)

"Road rage is the incredibly unbearable frustration of being unable to successfully make the switch from the electronic to the mechanical universe while driving. It happens outside the car all the time, under different names. ADD, Going Postal, and a host of other modern phenomena will undoubtedly one day be linked to this inability of the human species to click from "reality" to "simulated reality" seamlessly without any psychic scars. Road rage is the intense anger you feel at not being able to click out of the traffic jam you're stuck in. Without knowing why you're so angry, you feel trapped in your car, claustrophobic, and anything—including violence—is better than suffocating under those conditions of attendance."

Read Mercer Schuchardt,
New York University

"Anger is a killing thing: it kills the man who angers, for each rage leaves him less than he had been before—it takes something from him."

Louis L'Amour, author

"I have some road rage inside of me. Traffic, especially in Los Angeles, is a pet peeve of mine."

Katie Holmes, actress

"There's a level of resentment by some people who perceive because of the car you drive that you're also a certain kind of person."

Glenn Gillies, engineer

"There is nothing to suggest that road rage is distinct from any other form of anger. But for many of us, driving has become one of the most frustrating activities we are regularly engaged in."

Matthew Joint, head of behavioral analysis, The Automobile Association, group public policy road safety unit

"Have you ever noticed? Anybody going slower than you is an idiot, and anyone going faster than you is a maniac?"

George Carlin, comedian

"Driving is a social responsibility, not a social occasion."

Robert Bickers, author

Amazing Facts and Figures

- In 2003, the Canadian Psychiatric Association conducted a telephone study of drivers in order to determine who is most likely to "lose it" behind the wheel. They were hoping to determine the contributing psychological makeup of drivers most at risk of reacting violently with other drivers. Of the 2,610 people surveyed, 5.5 percent belonged to a group called "hard-core road ragers." It was determined that almost all of the people in this small group had some form of severe depression or anxiety and a diminished capacity to socialize. They concluded the most trigger-happy of offenders in road-rage incidents are predisposed to acts of aggression, regardless of whether they are on or off the highway.

- Between 1993 and 2003, the number of vehicles on the road in the province of Ontario, in central Canada, jumped nearly 50 percent.

- The city of Vancouver in British Columbia, Canada's western-most province, now has more cars per capita than does Los Angeles.

- As of 2002, the estimated economic cost of police-reported crashes involving drivers between the ages of 15 and 20 was $40.8 billion.

- A survey of Canadian drivers conducted by the Steel Alliance of Canada and the Canada Safety Council found drivers in the province of Alberta to be the most aggressive in the nation. Of those surveyed, 90 percent agreed that congestion feeds aggression and 42 percent admitted to feelings of road rage.

- According to David K. Willis, president of the AAA Foundation for Traffic Safety, "Vehicles and firearms are the principal weapons of choice during outbursts of road rage. In 35 percent of the incidents reviewed for our study, a vehicle was used as a weapon. In 37 percent, a firearm was used. But almost any conceivable kind of weapon can be wielded by enraged drivers."

- About 115 people die each day from traffic crashes in the U.S. Nearly 42,000 people die every year from traffic crashes, sending 4 million more to emergency rooms and hospitalizing 400,000, half with permanent disabilities. On-the-job traffic crashes cause 3,000 deaths, 332,000 injuries, and cost employers over $43 billion, according to NHSTA, and can reduce employee productivity by 40 percent.

AMAZING FACTS AND FIGURES

SYNOVATE STUDY

In July 2005, the polling firm Synovate conducted a global study, polling drivers from Greece, France, the United States, Brazil, Malaysia, India, Korea, Taiwan, South Africa, and the United Kingdom. They found drivers in the United Kingdom indulge in the highest number of rude behavior incidents, with 81 percent of drivers reporting having witnessed rude gestures and or verbal insults. South Africa came a close second at 71 percent, Greece registered third at 52 percent and the United States fourth, at 52 percent. Surprisingly, on a global scale, the United States scored lower than South Africa, the United Kingdom, and Greece in almost every area surveyed. A mere four percent of American drivers reported seeing aggressive behavior in which the other driver got out of their vehicle and threatened other drivers. South African drivers led all countries surveyed in overall road rage, with 64 percent admitting flashing headlights had perpetually blinded them. Still in South Africa, 67 percent admitted to having experienced aggressive and/or threatening driving behavior.

- The percentage of aggressive drivers in the United States has doubled from 22 percent in 1996 to 44 percent today, with about 82 percent of those saying their angry response is acceptable.

ROAD RAGE

BERT SPERLING'S TOP 10 MOST DIFFICULT CITIES TO NAVIGATE

1. Boston, Massachusetts
2. Washington, DC
3. San Francisco, California
4. Baltimore, Maryland
5. New York, New York–Northeastern New Jersey
6. Ft. Lauderdale–Hollywood–Pompano Beach, Florida
7. Los Angeles, California
8. Seattle–Everett, Washington
9. Providence, Pawtucket Rhode Island
10. Norfolk–Newport News–Virginia Beach, Virginia

Source: Bert Sperling, *America's Most Challenging Cities to Navigate*, www.bestplaces.net/docs/studies/NavCities.aspx

- In addition to the emotional toll, on-the-job traffic crashes annually cost employers about $3.5 billion in property damage, $7.9 million in medical care and emergency service taxes, $17.5 billion for wage premiums, $4.9 billion for workplace disruption (to hire and train either new employees or temporary employees) and $8.5 billion in disability and life insurance costs.

- "The Mizell research uncovered 10,037 incidents of violent aggressive driving between January 1, 1990, and August 31, 1996—the period studied. At least 218 men, women, and children were killed as a result of these incidents, and another 12,610 were injured."

- A 2004 Gallup poll cited in several newspapers, including the *New York Times,* stated that motorists were more worried about road rage (42 percent) than about drunk driving (35 percent).

Select Bibliography

James, Leon, and Diane Nahl. *Road Rage and Aggressive Driving: Steering Clear of Highway Warfare.* Amhurst, New York: Prometheus Books, 2000.

Rich, Curt. *Drive to Survive.* Osceola, WI: MBI Publishing Company, 1998.

Larson, John A. and Carol Rodriguez. *Road Rage to Road Wise.* New York, NY: A Forge Book, Tom Doherty Associates, Inc.,1999.

Web Sites

Drivers around the world share their experiences, and their outrage, online on web sites such as: *www.driveandstayalive.com, justrage.com, MonkeyMeter.com, roadragers.com, DrDriving.org.*

Acknowledgements

When I first began conducting research for this book, I had no idea what I was getting into. From the tragedy of the shootings in Boston, to the humor of *Monkeymeter.com*, I found the phenomenon of road rage endlessly fascinating. As a non-driver, I couldn't fathom how anyone in his or her right mind could become so enraged as to act violently toward another person. What I hadn't counted on discovering was the complexity of the driving experience, and just how many different elements are at play on the road at any one time. As Michael Zizzi so aptly points out, driving is really a conversation. The trouble is, we don't pay attention to what's being said until voices shout, horns blare, and fingers gesture.

I was also surprised to learn that road rage is largely a Western phenomenon. As I searched for stories in Japan, or Indonesia, or India, I found very few cases. When I searched the

United States, South Africa, and the United Kingdom, the results shocked me. In the most highly industrialized countries, the stress of day-to-day life seems almost too much to bear, and it would appear that people have reached the breaking point.

I'm indebted to the sociological and psychological perspective and insights provided by Dr. Leon James and Dr. David Lewis. I'm also grateful for the assistance and patience of Ellen Bryan and Kara Turner at Altitude Publishing while I flailed around with the wealth of information I came across on a daily basis. Thanks also to my editor, Deborah Lawson.

In addition, I would like to extend a hearty "Thank You!" to my long-suffering friends and family who endured my endless questions and longwinded stories about raging drivers.

I found no easy solutions to this issue, but I will say this: The next time I'm in a car with someone who is about to explode, I'm hopping out and walking.

Photo Credits

Cover: Comstock Images; page 8: AP Photo/The Brockton Enterprise, J. Kiely Jr.; page 9 top: AP Photo; page 9 bottom: AP Photo/Paul Sakuma; page 10: AP Photo/Tyler Morning Telegraph, Tom Worner; page 11: AP Photo/Scanpix Nordfoto, Keld Navntoft; page 12: AP Photo/Colin Braley, Pool; page 13: AP Photo/Amy E. Conn.

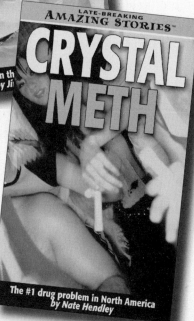

Killer Flu
by Jim Poling Sr.

Crystal Meth
by Nate Hendley

Wrongfully Accused

by Nora Rock

China: the Next Monster Power?

by Nate Hendley

Hurricane Hell

by Dee van Dyk

Water Matters

by Moushumi Chakrabarty

Inside the War in Afghanistan

by Sheila Enslev Johnston

Dangerous Dogs

by Roxanne Willems Snopek

Identity Theft
by Rennay Craats

Plastic Surgery Gone Wrong
by Melanie Jones